Eyewitness Accounts of the American Revolution

A Tour
through Part of
the North Provinces
of America

Patrick M'Robert

The New York Times & Arno Press

A TOUR

THROUGH PART OF THE

NORTH PROVINCES

OF

AMERICA:

BEING,

A Series of LETTERS wrote on the Spot,
in the Years 1774, & 1775.

TO WHICH ARE ANNEX'D,

TABLES, fhewing the Roads, the Value
of Coins, Rates of Stages, &c.

BY PATRICK M'ROBERT.

EDINBURGH: Printed for the Author. 1776.

OFFPRINT from *The Pennsylvania Magazine of History and Biography*, April, 1935

Published by

THE HISTORICAL SOCIETY OF PENNSYLVANIA

TABLE OF CONTENTS

PREFACE

THE only copy of Patrick M'Robert's *Tour* that the editor has seen is in the Treasure Room of the Harvard College Library,[1] and is herewith reproduced by the gracious permission of the library authorities. Of the author we know only that he was a well-educated Scot, of some means, who visited America in 1774 and 1775, probably with a view to settling there. The account is made up of seven letters, "wrote on the Spot," which were later gathered into a pamphlet and printed for the use of "those who have perhaps not had the opportunity of better intelligence."

The *Tour* is one of the very best in the travel literature of eighteenth century America. It is in many ways superior to Burnaby's account,[2] and far more reliable than the *Travels* of Peter Kalm.[3] The editor knows of no pre-revolutionary travel book which compares with this in acuteness of observation, or which exhibits a more "inviolable regard to truth." What M'Robert saw, he faithfully recounted; when he relied upon hearsay, he carefully noted that fact. His judgments were independent and judicious, notably in the conclusion that he reached concerning the character of the much-maligned Yankees: "The Rhode Islanders have pretty much the same dispositions as the New-Englanders, and from what I have seen of them, I am apt to believe that both get a worse character, than they generally deserve." Unlike Peter Kalm, and travelers of most ages, M'Robert did not lift his observations of the climate and soil of North America in large chunks from the works of his predecessors —he based them upon actual experience. Although M'Robert traveled through the Northern provinces on the eve of the Revolution, scant reference is made to the brewing of the momentous events

[1] There is another copy of the *Tour* in the John Carter Brown Library at Providence, and Mr. Lawrence Wroth informs me that a third copy was sold at the Anderson Galleries, April 18, 1921, for $355, going into private hands. It is thus evident that the pamphlet is both rare and valuable.

[2] Andrew Burnaby, *Travels through the Middle Settlements in North America (1759–1760)*, London, 1775.

[3] Peter Kalm, *Travels into North America (1748–1749)*, J. R. Forster, trans., 3 vols., Vol. I. Warrington, 1770; Vols. II. and III., London, 1771.

of that period. We catch a glimpse of the difficulties between the colonies and England in the letter from Nova Scotia, wherein he notes that "there are very few troops here at present, they being mostly gone to Boston," and in that from Rhode Island wherein he reported the inhabitants of Boston as having "high notions of liberty." But M'Robert turned the keen eye of a Scottish man of business upon the practical affairs of farming, industry, and commerce. These were his chief concerns and he deplored the "unhappy disputes" which promised to act as an embargo in closing to immigrants "the best country in the world for people of small fortunes."

The editorial notes have been inserted with the twofold purpose of amplifying the account and of providing a ready set of references by which the accuracy of the author's observations may be tested. The *Tour* is here reproduced exactly as it appears in the original; no changes in spelling or punctuation have been made. The editor wishes to express his gratitude to Mr. George Parker Winship for arranging for the photostat from which this edition is printed.

CARL BRIDENBAUGH

INTRODUCTION

The following Letters were wrote for the amusement of a particular friend, without the least intention of ever laying them before the publick. Had the writer ever dreamed of publishing this Tour thro' America, he might been much more minute in his enquiries and observations. He is now highly sensible of the many useful observations he has omitted, and passed by without notice. However, such as occurred to him most readily are here related in a plain simple stile, without any ornaments or flow of rhetoric, as he did not write for the literati who have access to better information, but only for the amusement of those who have perhaps not had the opportunity of better intelligence. On this account, he hopes to be indulged for any vulgarisms the reader may meet with in the stile. One thing he is conscious of, that he has had in all his relations an inviolable regard to truth; and if in any thing he may be wrong, it is from wrong information, and not from any intention of his own.

The misrepresentations and contradictory accounts received from that western world, since the spirit of emigration prevailed in North Britain, may perhaps apologize for publishing this Tour. For, while one represented the case of the emigrants as a state of perfect felicity, as if they had entered into elysium upon their setting foot on the American shore; another described it to be the most deplorable, as if when they crossed the Atlantic, they had plunged themselves into labyrinths of endless misery. These are only the relations of party and prejudice, and are exaggerated on both sides. For, as in this life, we need not expect uninterrupted prosperity in America more than in Europe, neither are they who have emigrated wretched to any degree like what has been represented. On the contrary, the writer of these Letters will venture to affirm, that it was the best country in the world for people of small fortunes; or in other words, the best poor man's country, before these unhappy disputes arose. It takes a good while however, to get established on an agreeable footing even in this country; the difficulties to encounter in America are many: in the first place, a long sea voyage, there every thing is strange; you have all to seek, and as it were, to begin the world a-new; to acquire acquaintances; to struggle hard for a character, &c. These require courage and resolution in the adventurer, and with a little share of these is easily overcome by young people, or by those who have emigrated from hardships at home; for men in this particular are like trees, they do not answer so well after a certain age for transplantation, nor do they do so well from a good soil as from a bad.

These Letters were wrote in the order they occurred, and are so given here without regard to method or regularity. As New York was the first part of the Tour, it is here first described; and so on as places came in the way. Accordingly, the first Letter, after a short history of the voyage, describes the city of New York, with parts adjoining. The second, gives an account of Hudson's river, the high lands, Albany, with some part of the country round; some further remarks on the province of New York, its laws, rates of provision, labour, produce, cattle, &c. Upon this province the writer has been more particular than on some of the rest; both because, as it is first treated of, it will serve to give the reader a more distinct notion of the country, and make him understand the better what follows, as many of the particulars related of New York are applicable to the other colonies; and, as he spent more time, he had access to be better informed, and make more observations there than in many of the other places thro' which he travelled.

His next course was towards Rhode Island, about 200 miles from New York, which, with some observations on Long Island, the Sound, Connecticut, with a short account of Boston and the province of Massachusetts Bay, &c. is the subject of the third Letter.

The next contains an account of Halifax, the province of Nova Scotia, its produce, trade, &c.

Next is a particular description of the Island of St John's.

Then his course was back thro' the wilds of Nova Scotia to Halifax, and thence to Philadelphia, which is described, its trade, Manufacturies, &c.

His next rout was thro' New Jersey, which he describes, with the several towns he passed on his return to New York.

The next gives a short account of the back part of the province of New York, where he made an excursion in the spring 1775. The rates of land and terms of settlement there, as well as in many other parts of the country, the customs, manner of living, &c. of the Indians.

To which is added very useful tables, shewing the distances of most of the noted places from one another in English miles, the rates of stages between New York and Philadelphia. The value of coins as they pass in the different provinces, thro' which the Tour lay.

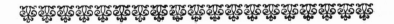

PATRICK M'ROBERT'S

Tour Through Part of the North Provinces of America

1774-1775

Edited by
CARL BRIDENBAUGH

LETTER I.

I Wrote you from Kirkcudbright, where we embarked the 6th of May last, bound for this port, where, after an agreeable passage, tho' tedious, we arrived the 18th July.

We met with nothing material on our passage; only a little girl of about nine years of age fell over board and was lost. Another, who had been sickly before she came on board, died. But to make amends for that loss, we had one born on board. The mother recovered so fast that she was on deck in three days. Excepting these, we all kept our health very well, after our sea sickness was over, which lasted with me three weeks. We were diverted on our passage by a kind of fish called Bonittes,[4] in shape like machrel, but larger, some thirty pounds weight, which followed our vessel for six weeks. We killed and eat so many that all hands began to tire of them. These, by chasing the flying fish, which sometimes fell on our decks, made us often good diversion; and, when the sword fish appeared, he afforded as good sport by chasing the Bonittes, which he never gave over till he had made his meal. We steered as far south as the 24th degree of latitude for the benefit of getting in to the Trade Winds. Here it was so hot, that, if any of us laid our hand on any iron about the vessel, we were soon obliged to remove it. We met with several sudden gusts of wind off Bermudas; but our mariners keeping a good look out, they happily did us no damage. The first land we made, was the high lands of the Jerseys, about ten or twelve miles to the south of Sandyhook, from Sandyhook to New York, is about thirty miles, having New Jersey and Staten Island on the west, and Long Island on the east, forms the mouth of Hudson's river, and harbour of New York. On both sides of the harbour, the woods, country houses, orchards, and fields of Indian corn, form at this season of the year a beautiful prospect. There is very good water up to New York, the harbour is spacious and large, with many convenient docks or quays, with store-houses upon them for vessels of any burden to

[4] Bonito; colloquially Bonita. A rich tasting fish similar to Bluefish.

1

lie always afloat along side of them.[5] Here are at present upward of 300 sail of shipping. They carry on an extensive trade from this port to Britain, Ireland, Holland, France, Spain, Portugal, up the Mediterranian, the West Indies, Spanish Main, as well as to the other colonies. Their exports are chiefly wheat, flour, Indian corn, indigo, flaxseed, pot and pearl ashes, fish, oil, pork, iron, timber, lumber, wax, and live cattle to the West Indies. Their imports are from Britain all kinds of cloth, linen and woolen, wrought iron, shoes, stockings, &c. From Holland, they have Europian and East India goods; from France, Spain and Portugal, wines, spirits, fruits, silks, and other articles of luxury; from the Spanish Main, they have logwood, mahogany, some indigo and dollars; from the West Indies, they have sugar, rum and molasses. Another considerable article of their export is built vessels, a good many of which are now on the stocks at this port, which they generally load with their own produce, and carry to some market where they sell both ship and cargo. They have great choice of wood in their ship-yards. Their upper timbers they make all of cedar, which they prefer to oak. They are very nice in the workmanship of ship-building here, and use a great deal of ornament and painting about the vessels.

This country was first settled by the Dutch in the year 1608,[6] who called New York, New Amsterdam, but King Charles the II. during the first Dutch war, 1664, granted New York, the Jerseys and Penselvania, to his brother James duke of York, who sent over a squadron of men of war, and land forces, who reduced New York; the other places settled by Dutch, and Swedes, also submitted: and, these countries were confirmed to the English by the Dutch, at the next treaty of peace between the two nations.

New York is situate about 41 degrees north latitude and 74 degrees west longitude from London, upon the south end of an island, of about fourteen or fifteen miles in length, and between two and three broad, formed by a branch of Hudson's river running into the

[5] These docks were located on the East River; the only docks on the Hudson River were the Albany Pier and the Corporation Dock, erected in 1750 and 1771. G. W. Edwards, *New York as an Eighteenth Century Municipality, 1731–1776* (New York, 1917), 152–153.

[6] Henry Hudson entered the North River in September, 1609, and the town of New Amsterdam was not planted until July, 1625. A. C. Flick, ed., *History of the State of New York* (10 vols., New York, 1933–), I. 159, 268.

east river, or Sound that divides Long Island from the continent. The situation is extremly pleasant, upon a rising ground from the shore or river on both sides. The city is large, and contains a great many neat buildings.[7] The publick buildings, and places of worship, are generally very neat, and well finished, if not elegant. The college,[8] tho' only one third of the plan is compleat, makes a fine appearance, on one of the finest situations perhaps of any college in the world. Here are taught divinity, mathematicks, the practice and theory of medicine, chymistry, surgery, and materia medica. One circumstance I think is a little unlucky, the enterance to this college is thro' one of the streets where the most noted prostitutes live. This is certainly a temptation to the youth that have occasion to pass so often that way.

The new hospital * tho' not quite finished is another fine building upon the same plan as the Royal Infirmary at Edinburgh. The goal makes a fine appearance without, and if as agreeable within, I do not wonder to hear of its being pretty full.[9] The city hall, the exchange, the workhouse, are all neat brick buildings.[10] Here are also neat barracks for about 500 men. They have three English churchs, three Presbyterian, two Dutch Lutheran, two Dutch Calvenists, all neat and well finished buildings, besides a French church, an Anabaptist, a Methodist, a Quaker meeting, a Moravian church, and a

[7] In 1776 the population of New York was estimated at 25,000 and the town was reported to contain 2500–3,000 buildings. E. B. Greene and V. D. Harrington, *American Population before the Federal Census of 1790* (New York, 1932), 102.

[8] King's College, now Columbia University, founded in 1754.

* This building was burnt in February 1774, when almost finished; however, the inhabitants set about repairing it again directly.

[9] The "New Goal" was built at the Fields in 1759, but M'Robert here probably refers to the Bridewell, which had been newly opened as a place to segregate debtors from hardened criminals. *Minutes of the Common Council of the City of New York, 1675–1776* (8 vols., New York, 1905), VIII. 114.

[10] The city hall was erected in 1700, at the corner of Broad and Wall Streets. In 1752 a voluntary subscription to which the Commonalty contributed heavily was raised to build an exchange. In 1754, the city took over the enterprise. The workhouse, opened in 1736, served as a house of correction for unruly servants and slaves, and as a workhouse for vagrants. J. G. Wilson, ed., *The Memorial History of New York* (4 vols., New York, 1892), II. 42; *Min. Com. Council*, V. 367–368, 408, 435; *New York Gazette, or The Weekly Post-Boy*, Feb. 11, 1764; *Colonial Laws of New York* (5 vols., Albany, 1894–1896), II. 355–357.

Jews synagogue.[11] There are many other fine buildings belonging to private gentlemen and merchants; but the streets are in general ill paved, irregular, and too narrow.[12] There are four market places, all well supplied with all kinds of provisions.[13]

They are pretty well supplied with fresh water from pumps sunk at convenient distances in the streets. Their tea water they get at present brought in carts thro' the streets from the suburbs of the city; but they are now erecting a fire engine for raising the spring into a reservoir, from whence, by pipes, they can convey it to any part of the city.[14] They are pretty well guarded against accidents from fire, by obliging every citizen to register their house, and for one shilling a vent yearly, to have them swept once a month. They have also a number of engines kept at convenient distances: to each of these is appointed a captain, and a certain number of men.[15] And when a fire happens, a premium is always allowed to the captain and his men who can first make their engines play upon the fire. By this precaution fire seldom happens, and by the proper disposition of the engines, when it does happen, it is seldom allowed to spread farther than the house it brakes out in.

The streets are agreeably shaded in some parts with trees.[16] They

[11] For descriptions of these churches, see *Memorial History of New York*, I. II. *passim.*

[12] "Sufficient Pebble Stones" were the principal paving material. The pavement sloped from the sides of the streets toward the center, which served as a gutter to carry off the water. Since 1766 the town had been active in paving, but still found much to be done. In 1775 John Adams spoke of the streets as "vastly more regular and elegant than those of Boston." *Works* (10 vols., Boston, 1850–1856), II. 347. Dr. Edwards thinks the streets were well cleaned after 1770. *New York, etc.,* 170.

[13] In 1774 there were at least six markets in use. Edwards, *op. cit.,* 71.

[14] The pump water was brackish, and drinking or tea water had to be procured in the suburbs from the "Tea Water Pump." The English engineer, Christopher Colles, persuaded the Common Council to construct a municipal water system. A reservoir of 20,000 hogsheads capacity served by a steam pump was built between Pearl and White Streets. It was covered to keep off the sun's rays which were believed to contaminate the water. The cylinder for the engine was cast in a local iron works. Fourteen miles of hollow log conduits were planned, and ordered from Albany, but the outbreak of hostilities prevented the completion of the scheme. *Min. Com. Council,* VIII. 26ff.; Edwards, *op. cit.,* 139–141; *New York Weekly Mercury,* Aug. 1, 1774.

[15] In 1772 New York boasted eleven fire companies and engines, with a force of 163 men superintended by the fire chief, Jacobus Stoutenburgh, and three engineers. Edwards, *op. cit.,* 136.

[16] The inhabitants living on Broadway were allowed to set out locust and beech trees in 1708. *Min. Com. Council,* II. 353.

have a fort, but of no great strength, and a battery with a good number of guns mounted, which may command that part of the harbour between New York and the Governor's Island. Near the fort is an equestrian statue of king George the III. upon an elegant pedestial in the middle of a fine green rail'd in with iron. At the crossing of two public streets, stands at full length a marble statute of lord Chatham erected by the citizens in gratitude for his strenuous opposition to the stamp act in 1766[17] They have several large roperies, distilleries, breweries, and a large iron work carried on here.[18] They have plenty of mechanicks of all kinds, by whom almost every thing that is made with you in Britain is made to as great perfection here.[19] The inhabitants are in general brisk and lively, kind to strangers, dress very gay; the fair sex are in general handsome, and said to be very obliging. Above 500 ladies of pleasure keep lodgings contiguous within the consecreated liberties of St. Paul's.[20] This part of the city belongs to the church, and has thence obtained the name of the *Holy Ground*. Here all the prostitutes reside, among whom are many fine well dressed women, and it is remarkable that they live in much greater cordiality one with another than any nests of that kind do in Britain or Ireland.

It rather hurts an Europian eye to see so many negro slaves upon the streets, tho' they are said to deminish yearly here. The city is governed by a mayor, and divided into seven different wards, over each of which an alderman and an assistant presides. They have generally the same laws and regulations as is in England. There are computed between twenty-six and thirty thousand inhabitants in the city; in this number are, I believe, included the slaves, who make at least a fifth part of the number.[21]

[17] The statue of George III. was on Bowling Green, and that of Pitt in Wall Street. 2 *Massachusetts Historical Society Proceedings,* IV. 291–298.

[18] The cylinder for the reservoir pump was cast at the foundry of Sharp and Curtenius, and was "allowed by the Judges to be extremely well executed." *Rivington's New York Gazetteer,* Feb. 16, 1775.

[19] This fact is borne out by the newspaper advertisements. See, for example, *New York Weekly Mercury,* July 18, 1768; Feb. 6, Aug. 10, 1769; for iron, woolen, and tobacco manufacturers.

[20] That prostitution was widespread may be seen from the accounts in the *New York Weekly Mercury,* July 23, 1753; *New York Post-Boy,* Mar. 28, April 4, 1768; and *passim.* The authorities found it very difficult to suppress.

[21] These figures are substantially correct. *Cf.* Greene and Harrington, *American Population,* 102*n.*

There are many fine country seats upon this island, where nature has done so much, art has had very little share in making them very agreeable. The soil is generally light and sandy, and in some parts rocky; but mostly well cultivated, and produces fine crops of wheat, Indian corn, and barley; but oats do not thrive well here.[22] They have their wheat and barley cut, and they are now (July 20) cutting some oats near the town. They are hoeing the Indian corn, the ears of the most foreward of which are just appearing: I am told it will not be ripe till October, this grain is a very strong grower; some of the heads, I believe, you have seen. It grows upon a strong hollow jointed stalk, like a reed, which rises to the height of seven or eight feet, the blades are a deep green, and broad, resembling sedge leaves, and make at this season a very luxuriant appearance. They plant this grain in little hillocks, about five feet distant one way, and three feet the other, having first laid a little dung, they plant two or three grains in a hill, and afterwards keep them clean by horse and hand hoeing. The time of planting is about the first of May. They often sow some melon, cucumber, or squash seed along with the Indian corn, which soon grows to perfection in the open fields. They generally have from 120 to 200 fold increase of this grain; but then a small quantity, one fourth of a bushel, plants an acre. They grind this grain into meal for feeding their negroes with. It is also very good, either ground or whole, for hogs, horses, fatting black cattle, or poultry.

Their horses here are not very large, about fourteen hands high, of a sharp boned make, but very hardy. A good one will sell from £ 10, to 20 sterling. The cows are of a middle size, of the long horned kind, bare haird, not very neat, but good milkers. A good one will cost from £ 3, to 5 sterling. I have seen no polled cows here.[23] Their sheep are a kind of half mugs,[24] too long leged, though their wool and mutton are both pretty good. A sheep sells from 6, to 10 s. sterling. Their hogs are much of the same kind, that you have in Britain, but make exceeding sweet pork. Their poultry are very good, large and fat.

[22] These farms, it must be noted, were located near the city, and were superior to those farther inland. The New York market influenced them greatly. P. W. Bidwell and J. I. Falconer, *History of Agriculture in the Northern United States* (Washington, 1925), 89–90.

[23] Cows whose horns have been cut off.

[24] A breed of sheep having the face completely covered with wool.

LETTER II.

From New York, we imbarked on board a sloop bound for Albany, which is between 160, and 170 miles distant. The course is mostly north, the river being pretty straight. This river is from one to three miles broad below the high lands, which are forty miles from New York. The banks on the west-side are steep and rocky for near twenty miles; after that, you see a good country on both sides for several miles, till you come to the entrance of the high lands.[25] Here the river is contracted to about a quarter of a mile in breadth, and guarded, as it were by rocky precipices, one would think, hanging over their head some hundred fathoms high. Here the ragged rocks covered with trees hanging over the river below, the vessels under sail, as it were starting from some cavern of the shaggy rocks, the rivulets powring down from such an immense height, form, perhaps, one of the grandest landscaps in nature. These ragged mountains continue for about twelve miles; then we came into a tolerable level country, and the river extends to its usual breadth. Several pleasant country seats are to be seen on both sides; here, on the west bank of the river is a little town called Windsor, having a good quay, and large granaries, and stores for holding the grain of the adjacent country,[26] where it is brought to be sent to New York for exportation. They have also many landing places, at convenient distances up the river, where granaries are built for the same purposes; here the country people for thirty or forty miles bring their wheat on sleighs or sledges on the snow in the winter. A pair of their horses will draw thirty bushels of wheat in one of these sledges thirty miles upon the snow, and return the same day. We passed many fine country-seats, and orchards, within view from the river; we had also a view of the Blue or Catskill mountains, but at a great distance: and after a fine passage of twenty seven hours we arrived at Albany. This is a considerable large town, or city as they would have it called,[27] built on the west-side of Hudson's river, on the declivity of a hill. The houses are mostly brick; but of an old fashioned make with their

[25] The Palisades.

[26] Windsor: the seat of the Clinton family.

[27] Albany had been granted a city charter by Governor Dongan. In 1776 the town contained 350 houses, or about 2800 inhabitants. Greene and Harrington, *American Population,* 102n.

gables to the streets. There is here an English church, a high and low Dutch church, with a Presbyterian meeting-house. The streets are very dirty; they have a fort that overlooks the town, but in bad repair. Their hospital[28] has been a spacious wooden building, in a fine airy situation; but is now almost uninhabitable. The barracks are in the same condition. To this place belong about fifty sloops from fifty to eighty tons each, employed constantly on the river in carrying down wheat, pease, boards, and other lumber to New York.[29] They likwise have three vessels in the West I[n]dia trade, and one that trades to London.

The inhabitants are mostly of Dutch extraction, whose language and manners they in a good measure retain, tho' they can mostly speak English. They are a heavy and dull people, at least they appear so to me. They are said to be very honest, tho' not the most hospitable; nor will they easily be persuaded to accommodate you with what you want, when in their taverns.

The soil is very indifferent for several miles near Albany, being nothing but a cold spungy clay or sand, covered with pine trees; but even upon this soil they have exceeding good crops when they are at any pains to manure their land, as Mr. Tuniclif a Derbyshireman has showen, who settled here about five years ago on one of the worst spots in this country, and by his managment had this year the best crops I have seen. His stock is also of a superior kind to any in the country. He got the breed of his sheep from Derbyshire. The harvest is at least a fortnight later here than at New York. The woods abound with huckle-berries, goose-berries, straw-berries, black-berries, cran-berries, &c. and apples, and wild grapes.

In the river are caught several sorts of fish, particularly sturgeon, and in the spring vast shoals of a kind of herrings, which are taken many miles above this town.

The Weather is sensibly colder here than at New York, where it is very hot at this season of the year, for six weeks or two months. The river is also frozen over for perhaps three months in winter, which is scarcely ever the case at New York. Indian corn and grass

---

[28] On October 4, 1775, the Provincial Congress ordered the local committee at Albany to put the hospital and barracks in a state of repair. Joel Munsell, *Annals of Albany* (10 vols., Albany, 1850–1859), VIII. 226.

[29] In 1769, Albany boasted "31 sloops . . . , which carry from 400 to 500 Barrels of Flour each, trading constantly from thence to York, & they make Eleven or 12 Trips a year each." Quoted in Bidwell and Falconer, *History of Agriculture*, 140.

seem to thrive rather better here than at New York. The soil or climate seems also more favourable for oats. We made some little excursions into the country to the westward of Albany, where the soil after a few miles, mends; and you come into very good land, and thriving settlements. They have a great many saw-mills erected for working their pine into boards, which they send down the river to New York.

After a few days stay, we embarked again for New York: our vessel running aground about 12 miles below Albany, we went ashore: Here we found plenty of apples and cherries in the woods, fine water and timber, plenty of mellons cucumbers, squashes, &c. and some little plantations of tobacco. For this plant they prepare the land the same way you do for cabbages. They sow the seed in the spring, and transplant in May or June into rows of four feet distance, hand hoeing and keeping them very clean: the plants grow till September, when they are ready to take up. At about ten miles further down the river, we went ashore and saw them make pot and pearl ashes. About forty miles further down we went ashore, where they have many lime-stone quarries: We saw fifteen or sixteen kills all burning at once. I observe all above the high lands but getting in their crops (Aug. 10), but those below have them all in a week ago. They have a great advantage over you here in point of climate. Their grain is far more thoroughly dried than you can get it. This makes it both keep better and grind cleaner. They often throw 10,000 bushels of it into the hold of a vessel to lie for a two or three months voyage, without receiving any damage. Tradesmen and labourers wages are high in all the province: a joiner six shillings a-day, a mason or brick-layer the same, and other trades in proportion, but they must be good hands, else they won't get employ till they go to the back settlements.

Labourers have their three and four shillings a-day about New York; but at present they seem rather overstocked, owing to the arrival of so many adventurers from Britain and Ireland; they tell me that no less than twenty two vessels have arrived at New York with passengers within these twelve months.[30] There is plenty of room and employ for them in the back countries, where many of them are gone.

[30] Compare, *New-York Mercury*, January 3, 1774; *Rivington's New-York Gazetteer*, January 6, 13; May 27, 1774; for Scots' servants for sale.

All necessaries of life are plenty, and reasonable; For example, beef at four and five pence the pound; good mutton the same; a good hen at a shilling, and pork and veal in proportion; butter sixteen pence the pound; the best flower, seventeen shillings the hundred weight; West India rum from three shillings and six pence, and three and nine pence the gallon. Rum distilled here, at two and six pence the gallon; beer, and all sorts of wines, about the same prices that you have them at; cyder, four pence the bottle. The only dear drink is London porter, which is two shillings the bottle. Observe, that in all the above rates and prices, I speak of the currency of the country, which is in proportion as seven pence sterling to a shilling.

The most current coins here in gold, are the Johanneses, half and quarter; the moidore, with some guineas; in silver, the Spanish dollar, the half, quarter, and eighth of a dollar, which last is their shilling. They have also some British shillings circulating. Their market of meat and butter must this season of the year be over early; for neither of them will keep long. They are very well supplied with fresh fish, such as cod, sturgeon, black fish and flounders, at two pence per pound; lobsters, and other shell fish in great plenty.

This country is not less happy in its mineral than vegetable productions, having great plenty of iron and copper; some lead and silver mines wrought to great advantage. The whole province is divided into twelve counties, each of which sends two representatives to their assembly, which meets annually at New York. They have a governor and council appointed by his Majesty: These with the assembly, frame laws for the province, the same as your houses of parliament do in Britain; but their laws must all be sent over and approven of by his Majesty before they have their proper force. The assembly have the power of imposing taxes and rates upon the province; also of imposing duties on goods imported from any of the other colonies, or on any commodity that does not interfere with the trade of Great Britain. Besides this council and assembly, there is a superior court kept here, where three judges preside. Before this court are tried by jury all cases of life and death. They have also inferior courts, or courts of session and common pleas, in every county, for the trial of ordinary causes. Besides these, justices of the peace are appointed in every township, invested with the same powers as in England.

LETTER III.

Long Island is part of the province of New York, situated along the coast, opposite to the provinces of New York and Connecticut, being separated by a narrow sound, not more than half a mile over in some parts, by the New Yorkers called the East River. The island is about 130 miles in length, and about thirty broad. Opposite New York is a village and ferry half a mile over, where six ferry boats ply constantly.[31] In sight of New York are several fine country seats, and the whole island, as far as our little tour extended (which was only a few miles) exhibits to our view a pleasant diversity of houses, orchards, fields of Indian corn, hay and pasture. The soil is in general light, but the growth of every thing very luxuriant. As we passed along the road, we were delighted with the fine appearance of fruits of various kinds hanging over our heads.

Upon this island is a fine plain of several miles, where they tell us never a tree has grown. This is such a curiosity in this country that most travellers go to see it; but as we had engaged a passage we could not wait. A great many of the old settlers here are of Dutch extract, and very rich, said to be great hoarders; for, if a piece of gold or a dollar fall into their hands, it is ten to one if ever it sees the air again in their day. This hoarding disposition is natural to all the Dutch in this country. Returning again to New York we embarked on board a schooner for Rhode Island. Our course was along the sound or east river where a strong current sets eastward with the flowing sea, and the contrary with the ebb. About fourteen miles from New York, the sound is contracted to less than a quarter of a mile, with winding rocks on both sides, having several reefs of blind rocks running in below the water: here is a vast current, so agitated by the different reefs of rocks, that it forms a dangerous whirl-pool, where it is not uncommon for vessels that venture through at an improper time of the tide, or without a skilful pilot, to be caught in the eddy, and whirled round and round till they are dashed against some of these rocks: from hence, I suppose, and from its frightful appearance, it has obtained the name of *Hell's Gates.* But,

[31] Brooklyn. For an account of the ferries, see Edwards, *New York as an Eighteenth Century Municipality,* 172–183.

at the high water, and when the wind is favourable, they pass without danger, there being water enough for the largest vessel.

Here the branch of Hudson's river, that I mentioned before, to form the island of New York, joins the sound. While waiting for a proper time to pass these straits, we went ashore upon Long Island, and had a view of another part of the island which seems to be much like what I have already described for soil and productions; and as we sailed along the sound for forty miles, we had a view of both shores, with many pleasant country houses and orchards. Afterward, the sound is wider, and we had an imperfect view of the shore of the continent, keeping Long Island shore aboard: the wind being contrary we put into New Haven, the capital of Connecticut.[32] This is a pleasant town, hath four churches, the streets are regular and wide, has a pretty good harbour, tho' something open to the east. Here lie a good many small vessels. This province has its name from a river of that name which runs through it, and is navigable for ninety miles up the country. There are settlements upon this river for 300 miles up, with many little towns. They carry on a considerable trade to the West Indies, and the other colonies. They are mostly Independents, keen anti-government men, and said to be rather sharpers in trade. Here they build a good many vessels for sale. In the country they have large dairies of cows, and make good butter and cheese. Next morning we took our leave of this town, and before night, were abreast of Fishers Island, situate in the mouth of the sound between the east end of Long Island and the main land. Between these two islands also runs a very strong current, called the *Horse Race;* but not so dangerous as Hell's Gates. We rolled about in a great sea, and no wind all night after we had passed the Horse Race, and at day-break were in sight of the island of Romansland upon our starboard, and the coast of New England on our larboard.[33] The country is clear as far as we could see, and many ricks of hay standing on the fields. Near the entrance of Newport harbour stands a light house.[34] The mouth of the harbour is about half a mile over, with bold rocky shores on both sides. There is plenty of

[32] For an intimate picture of New Haven at this time, consult L. H. Gipson, *Jared Ingersoll* (New Haven, 1920), 16–34.

[33] By "Romans-land," M'Robert must mean Rhode Island.

[34] Beaver-Tail Light, erected in February, 1749. Richard M. Bayles, *History of Newport County, Rhode Island* (New York, 1888), 47.

water for the largest vessels; and after you come within Connanicut island, the harbour opens wide and spacious,[35] with good water all the way up to Providence, being thirty miles. A little within the mouth of the harbour, and opposite to Newport, is an island where stands a fort, which, if finished and properly garrisoned, may command the mouth of the harbour, and all along the quays of Newport.[36] The main street of Newport is a mile in length,[37] having several other streets branching out from it; the buildings are pretty good, some of stone, and some of brick, and some wood.[38] They carry on a considerable trade here to Europe, the coast of Africa, and the West Indies: they also fit out yearly a number of vessels, both for the cod and whale fishery.[39] Here lies at this time, upwards of a hundred sail of vessels. They have two English churches, two Presbyterian churches, a Quaker meeting, a Jewish synagogue, &c.[40] The face of the country is very pleasant, having many gentle rising hills of no great height: 'tis a pretty good soil, but stoney in some parts. They have made their divisions of stone walls, which are the first of the kind I have seen in America. They grow pretty good wheat, and Indian corn and rye here, with some barley, and oats; but they rather choose to graze their lands on this island than raise grain, as they

[35] Newport harbor was the best all-weather haven in New England; as James Birket noted in 1750, it was so conveniently located that "vessels are out or in, in a Moment." C. M. Andrews, ed., *Some Cursory Remarks Made by James Birket in His Voyage to North America, 1750–51* (New Haven, 1916), 29.

[36] Fort George, on Goat Island. See Charles Blaskowitz' Map of Newport, 1770, in John Carter Brown Library. "The[y] have abundance of good wharves which Extend the whole length of the town where vessels of any burthen can Load, discharge, or heave down without the help of Lighters." Birket, *Some Cursory Remarks*, 29.

[37] Thames Street.

[38] The finest buildings in Newport were Trinity Church, the Colony House, and the three masterpieces of Peter Harrison: The Synagogue, the Market, and the Redwood Library. See the artistic photographs in Kenneth Clark's *Architectural Monograph on Newport* (*White Pine Series*, VIII. no. 3, St. Paul, 1922). With a population of about 12,000, Newport was the fourth largest town in the colonies. Edward Peterson, *History of the Island of Rhode Island and Newport* (New York, 1853), 247.

[39] The principal trade was with the West Indies, traffic to Europe and Africa being much smaller in volume. Bruce M. Bigelow, "Aaron Lopez: Colonial Merchant of Newport," *New England Quarterly*, IV. 770–772. Evidence of the spermaceti candle business will be found in the *Newport Mercury*, August 26, 1771; January 2, 1774; and 7 Mass. Hist. Soc., *Collections*, IX. 88–92, 97–100.

[40] There were also Sabbatarian and Moravian congregations, and two Baptist churches. M'Robert is in error when he notes two Anglican churches; there was only one. Ezra Stiles, *Literary Diary* (F. B. Dexter, ed., 2 vols., New Haven, 1901), I. 61*n.*, 85.

think it more profitable. Their cattle are large; and they work their land mostly with oxen, a good pair of which will sell at eighty dollars, and will weigh about eighty stone a-piece, when fat. The cows are large and cheap; you may buy a good one for twenty or twenty two dollars. Their sheep are of a large kind, long legged, the wool very good. Here are several distilleries and ropperies, &c. carried on.[41] They have rum and other spirits much about the same rates as at New York. Their market[42] is also supplied with all kinds of provisions about the same prices. Fish are plenty, and rather cheaper than at New York. Fruits are plenty, tho' not in such abundance as to the south; they have also great plenty of cucumbers, melons, squashes, &c. growing in the fields.

They have a governor, council and assembly, and the same laws and regulations here as in New York. They have two denominations of currency, *viz.* Old tenor, and lawful money. Old tenor is of very small value; a pound is only equal to about eighteen pence sterling. Lawful money wants just a fourth of sterling in value. A pound lawful is equal to fifteen shillings sterling.[43] The coins current are the same as at New York.[44]

We intended to have gone by land to Boston, which is about fifty miles distant; but meeting with a vessel bound for Halifax in Nova Scotia, I will not have the opportunity of seeing Boston; but shall write you a few particulars of what I have heard of that province from pretty good information, *viz.*

Boston contains eighteen or twenty thousand inhabitants; is governed by seven men chosen yearly, called *select men.*[45] In the town used to be a militia regiment of twelve companies, a troop of

[41] There were at least twelve distilleries located around the Cove. Peterson, *History of the Island of Rhode Island,* 83.

[42] An extended account of the building of the market is in *Newport Mercury,* May 4, 1772.

[43] The gyrations of the badly managed Rhode Island currency are described by E. R. Potter and S. R. Rider, "Bills of Credit or Paper Money of Rhode Island," *Rider's Historical Tracts,* No. 8.

[44] The usually observant M'Robert failed to report the importance of Newport as a health resort. At the time of his visit, there were at least seventy-eight residents of South Carolina, Georgia, Jamaica, and Pennsylvania spending the summer at Newport. Carl Bridenbaugh, "Colonial Newport as a Summer Resort," R. I. Hist. Soc., *Collections,* XXVI. 23.

[45] Newport was also governed by the town meeting system.

horse guards, a company of cadets, a company and train of artillery, all militia. Thus you see they have had a martial spirit for some time; but now they may all be called militia who are fit to bear arms: for every one is obliged to provide himself with gun and bayonet, with belt and cartouch box, and appear at the review every day under the penalty of a severe fine.[46] The council is composed of twenty eight members, chosen by the house of assembly. The house of assembly consists of about 129 members, sent from the different counties and towns; of these Boston sends four. They have also a superior court where five judges preside; each county has also a court of common pleas, and there are said to be five hundred justices of the peace in the colony. There are about four hundred religious assemblies in the province, mostly Independents, some Presbyterians, some Baptists, and Quakers; only about twelve English churches in the whole province.

They have a college at Cambridge, about four miles from Boston, where divinity, mathematics, philosophy, and the oriental languages are taught. This college was founded above one hundred years ago. There are only three custom-houses in the province, at Boston, Salem, and Falmouth. The province of Massachusets is divided into fourteen counties, and is said to contain about three hundred thousand inhabitants.

Boston harbour is a very good one, and they used to carry on a very extensive trade wherever they could sell their commodities, which are fish, oil, and rum of their own distilling, pot and pearl ashes, lumber, flax-seed and shipping, &c. There have been 700 vessels clear'd out from this port in a year, and near as many entered inwards. The inhabitants are said to be rather keen, and will not stand to over-reach in trade when in their power; are great pretenders to sanctity, and have high notions of liberty. They have been great adventurers in trade, and generally successful; they are very inquisitive, want to know every circumstance relating to any stranger that comes amongst them, so that a traveller lately in that country had been so pestered with their idle queries, that, as soon as he entered a tavern, he used to begin and tell them, he was such a one, telling his name, travelling to Boston, born in North Britain, aged

---

[46] As the Boston Port Bill went into effect on June 1, 1774, M'Robert was unable to visit the Bay town.

about thirty, unmarried, prayed them not to trouble him with more questions but to get him something to eat: this generally had the desired effect.[47]

The Rhode Islanders have pretty much the same dispositions as the New Englanders, and from what I have seen of them, I am apt to believe that both get a worse character, than they generally deserve.[48]

[47] On the whole, Patrick M'Robert's reporter gave him a truthful account of Boston, and since he submits his description as hearsay, it has not seemed necessary to edit this portion of the narrative.

[48] This is good evidence of the author's independent judgment.

LETTER IV.

Dated Pictou, Nova Scotia, Sep. 1774.

From Rhode Island, we sailed for Halifax, on board a schooner bound for that port. Meeting with nothing remarkable, except that, upon the eighth day of our passage, the weather being foggy, as it generally is on these coasts, we fell in amongst rocks, and very narrowly escaped being cast away near the Seal Islands; but the weather clearing, we met with some New England fisher-men, who gave us directions how to steer clear of the rocks: so, in two days more, we got a-breast of Cape Sambers light-house,[49] amusing ourselves with fishing cod, which are very plenty and good upon these coasts.

The mouth of Chebucto bay, or Halifax harbour, is formed by Cape Sambero head upon the west, and Cornwallis island on the east: the entrance at first is three or four miles over, but grows narrower to about a mile. The course is north eight miles to Halifax. This is a very safe and commodious harbour: a little below Halifax is George's island, a pleasant little spot where is a guard-house, battery, and centries always kept, that take account of all vessels as they sail in or out of this harbour. There are two or three batteries with guns placed upon them along-side of the harbour, but rather out of repair.[50]

The town is pleasantly situated on the west-side of the harbour, upon the declivity of a pretty high hill, on the top of which is a guard-house and centries kept. A good deal has been done towards fortifying the hill, but not compleated. The plan of the town is very regular; the streets cross each other at right angles, by which it consists of many little squares.[51] The streets are not paved, but laid with good stones and gravel, which seem to make a better street than most pavements do. The buildings are mostly all wood, some few of stone; many of the wood seem to be going to decay, so that I suppose they will all build with stone when they come to rebuild them

[49] Cape Sambro lighthouse was erected in 1759 at a cost of £ 1,000, which were raised by a public lottery. T. D. Aikin, *History of Halifax City, Nova Scotia* (Nova Scotia Historical Society, *Collections,* 1895, III. 32, 51).

[50] On the fortifications, see A. W. H. Eaton, "Halifax Defences," in *History of Halifax* (Collection of Articles from *Americana,* in Harvard Library), and Aikin, *Halifax,* 209–211.

[51] The town, as it was a government enterprise, was carefully planned and laid out by Army engineers in 1749. Each square or block was 320 feet long by 120 feet deep. The streets were fifty-five feet in breadth. Aikin, *Halifax,* 10.

again.[52] Here is a neat English church, a Presbyterian meeting-house, and a Dutch meeting-house.[53] The town is above a mile in length, and three or four streets broad in some parts; it contains upwards of six thousand inhabitants.[54] At the upper end of the town is his Majesty's dock-yard inclosed with a strong stone wall, except on that side that touches the harbour.[55] Here are large stores for supplying the ships of war upon the American station; also a number of carpenters, and other artificers, kept in readiness to make any necessary repairs, being the only dock-yard in North America: here are large and convenient barracks for above a thousand men; but there are very few troops here at present, they being mostly gone to Boston. The trade of this port does not seem to be very extensive: there are not above thirty vessels here at present, and most of these are fishing schooners. They carry on a little trade to the West Indies, Philadelphia, and New York, where they send their fish and oil, and some furr and lumber: they have also a vessel or two that trades constantly to London.[56] They have several breweries and distilleries, and are famous for tanning the best leather in America.

Their currency is only of a tenth less value than sterling. *i. e.* 10 pounds Halifax, is equal to £ 9 sterling. The same coins pass amongst them that do in the other colonies: they have rather more British coins, owing to the large supplies of cash that have been sent over here by government, and laid out in repairing the harbour, building docks and batteries, opening streets and roads, &c. I am told, there is still about £ 3,000 per annum sent over here, and expended as the governor pleases; without these annual supplies from

[52] Since the majority of the first settlers had been brought over from the British Isles, they were unaccustomed to building with timber, and met with great difficulties in erecting their homes. The problem was solved by importing frames for the houses from Boston—even for St. Paul's Church. Aikin, *Halifax*, 10–11, 22.

[53] St. Paul's (Anglican), 1750; Protestant Dissenting Chapel (Mather's), 1750; and St. George's (Dutch), 1752. Most authorities have held that Mather's church was primarily congregational until well after the Revolution, but M'Robert indicates presbyterian control at an earlier date, and does not label it "independent" as was his custom with congregational churches.

[54] According to a public survey, the population in 1769 was about 5,000. Aikin, *Halifax*, 60. M'Robert's figures would, therefore, seem to represent a normal increase.

[55] Halifax was the northern port of the ships on the American station.

[56] There was a considerable trade between Newport and Halifax, indications of which occur in the *Newport Mercury* after 1768. Before the Port Bill, there was a fair amount of traffic with Boston.

home, this colony could not have subsisted in its infancy. The town was mostly built at the government's expence, about twenty-five years ago, and the first adventurers were brought over free.[57] Notwithstanding all these encouragements, the soil about this place is so very rocky that cultivation has not extended far from the town: however, there are a good many neat inclosures near the town, cleared and fenced, (with the stones that have been taken off the land,) which produce very good crops of wheat, rye, or oats, and very good clover and rye-grass hay. Indian corn does not seem to thrive here; their potatoes are very good, and all kinds of pulse and roots thrive well. Fruits are but scarce yet, as not many orchards are come to perfection, but those that have been planted seem to thrive, tho' the soil be stoney. The cleared lands run naturally to white clover, and in time, I believe, will make very good sheep pasture; but the stones will for ever be a bar to tillage.

Their horses are not very large, but handsome, and very hardy, and sell pretty high: a good one will cost £ 15, or 20. The black cattle are much of the size and make of good Galloway beasts, and every bit as well haired; sell pretty high: a good cow will cost £ 6, or 7.

Their sheep are rather less than to the south-ward, but dearer, sell about 14, or 15 shillings a-piece. The markets are higher here than in any other part of America: beef, five or six pence *per* pound; mutton, the same; salt pork, six pence. Butter is very good, sells at eight pence *per* pound; fish are very plenty and cheap.[58]

Their houses are mostly covered with shingles instead of slates; these are thin boards of about eighteen or twenty inches long, and four or five broad, nailed on in the same manner that slates are: A good cover of them will last forty or fifty years. They have also some houses covered with tiles.

They have a governor and council appointed by his Majesty, and an assembly of deputies sent from the different townships in the province, who meet annually at Halifax, and proceed much in the

[57] Christopher Kilby's itemized account for £ 173,938 . 2 . 3., expended in 1749, which he submitted to the Board of Trade, is printed by Aikin, *Halifax,* appendix D.

[58] There was only one market in Halifax in 1774. It was of frame construction, and had been erected in 1750 to serve both as a market and merchant's exchange. Aikin, *Halifax,* 25, 216.

the east shore; but upon the Bay of Fundy, in the inland country, and along the Gulph of St Laurence, are many large tracts of fine land, and the best grazing country I have seen in America.

The trade of the province is but small: they export fish, oil, lumber, furr and skins, with some live cattle.

The country abounds in deer of the large moose and Caribee[64] kinds, which the Indians kill and exchange their skins and venison with the settlers, for powder and shot, coarse blanketing, rum, &c. Round the coasts, and along the lakes of this country, are vast quantities of wild fowls, particularly geese, duck, brant, &c. the feathers of which afford an article of export.

They have lime-stone and coal in many parts of this country, and have lately found iron.

The climate is very healthy; the summer is not so warm as to the south, but the winters are sharper, tho' not so sharp as I have heard them represented. The snow generally fall[s] about Christmass, and lies till March. During this time the air is commonly clear, and serene, but it freezes keen at night. I have heard it said, that this country is buried in fogs for most part of the year: this is a great mistake; for no country has a clearer air than this, tho' the seas along the coast are often covered with a very thick fog.

[64] Caribou.

LETTER V.

Island of St John's.

From Pictou I embarked for the island of St John's,[65] which is but a few leagues distant. This island is situated in the Gulph of St Lawrence, between forty six and forty seven degrees of North Latitude, and about the sixty second and sixty third degrees of west longitude from London, is about one hundred and twenty miles in length, and thirty in breadth. We landed at Fort Amherst, which stands upon a rising ground, at the mouth of the harbour of Charlotte-town called by the French, *Port la Joy.* This fort is going to ruin: there are still twelve or fourteen guns mounted, a magazine, and barracks for a good number of men. Charlotte-town is the seat of the governor, and capital of the island, very pleasantly situated; but in its infancy, having only about fourteen or fifteen dwelling houses. The plan of the town, however, is very regular, and many have taken lots to build upon; so that, I have no doubt, but some time hence, it will form as fine a city as many in America.

The harbour is formed by the junction of three rivers, *viz.* The East, or Hillsborcugh river; the North, and the West rivers.[66] The first of these is navigable about twelve miles above the town, and the West river about as far. All these rivers join between Charlotte-town and the fort, which are very pleasantly situated upon two opposite points of land. There is very good water for the largest vessels, the harbour being about 6 or 7 fathoms deep, and large enough for all the navy of Great Britain.

From Charlotte-town, I went thro' woods, and a very level country (as most part of the island is) for eighteen miles to the north coast of the island. The road has been but lately opened. Here, at Little Rustico,[67] is a settlement, and a good deal of clear land, with good grazing for cattle: here is also a pretty good harbour, and little fishing shallops, but not water for any large vessel. Here I saw very good turnip, and cabbages. From this to Great Rustico, we travelled

[65] St. John's Island was renamed Prince Edward Island in 1790. A. B. Warburton, *History of Prince Edward Island* (St. John, N. B., 1923), 248.
[66] The North and West Rivers are now the York and the Elliot respectively.
[67] A fishing village founded by Pierre Rassicot in 1724. Warburton, *Prince Edward Island,* 40.

about six miles along a sandy flat shore: here is a tolerable good harbour for small vessels, a good deal of settlers, mostly French, and a considerable fishery carried on.

From this we travelled along the shore, which rises into headlands, or bluffs, as they are called here; some of them thirty or forty feet above high water: the faces of these are mostly red free stone, and stand perpendicular over the water. Under the most of these one can pass dry at low water. Upon the top of these free rocks is a surface of two or three feet deep of good soil, upon which I saw some very good cabbages and potatoes grow without dung. Upon the road we halted at a gentleman's house who had been an officer in the army: he has some very good wheat, and excellent garden stuffs. From this house our road lay along a sandy bush [beach?] for four miles to Little Harbour, or Grenville Bay, which we passed over in a boat to New London, a little town a-building on the west side of the harbour: it is only of a year's standing, has about a dozen houses in the form of a street, and a good many more scattered up and down near the harbour, which is a pretty safe one; has eleven feet water over the bar at low water. Here is a large store kept, all kinds of goods sold, and many fishing vessels employed. They export fish, oil, and timber, from this port to England, the West Indies, and up the Mediterranean. They have lately erected a sawmill here for making boards, as well as in several other parts of the island. After two days stay with Mr Clark the hospitable Quaker, who promotes this settlement, I travelled along the shore twelve miles farther to Malpique.[68] The shore is the same as to soil and appearance as that between and Rustico. We met with some gentlemens houses on our way and an old French settlement, where is a good deal of clear ground, and some houses standing. At Melpique are a good many French families, and a number of Scots settled. Here are about four thousand acres reserved for building a town upon, to be called Prince Town.[69] A good part of the ground where the town is to stand is clear, and some of the streets marked out, and some

[68] Malpeque was the principal village of the Micmac Indians on the island, and became a European settlement when three Acadian families came there in 1728. Warburton, *Prince Edward Island*, 41.

[69] Princetown, Georgetown, and Charlottetown were all surveyed and laid out in May, 1768, by order of Lieutenant-Governor Francklin. The former was the principal haven of the north shore fishing fleet.

houses a-building. Here is a harbour, rather wide, but tolerably safe, being guarded from the sea by several islands. Here also is carried on a considerable fishery.

From this place, I embarked with a guide on board a little boat, sailed eight miles south to the head of this bay or harbour, and landing, walked across the island, which is only two miles over here, and went to view an estate on the south west of the island, situated upon Bedaque bay, opposite to Malpique. Here is a good deal of very fine meadow, an old French settlement with a church and a mill, but all gone to ruin.

Bedeque is a very good harbour on the south-side of the island, having four fathoms water, and guarded from the sea by Indian Island, an island of about one hundred acres, a good part of which is meadow ground: most of the land that has been clear'd by the French is overgrown again with wood, except some spots which have very fine grass, and large quantities of fine marsh, that are covered with very high tides, where is excellent grass. Here are vast flocks of wild geese, brant, duck, &c. with numbers of seals and sea cows; also foxes and otters.

There being but one settlement farther west upon the island, and that but a small one, I returned again to Charlotte-town, by Tracadie, a settlement of the Macdonalds from the north of Scotland; here are about thirty families settled about two years ago, and doing well. They have a very good harbour, and are conveniently situated for the fishery: here they caught above forty barrels of eels this summer and sent to Quebec: there is also very good grazing for cattle.

At Charlotte-town I viewed the governor's field of experiment; in this little field he has very fine crops of wheat, clover, turnip, pease, beans, cabbages, carrots, potatoes, &c. No soil appears fitter for cultivation than this island. I also went and viewed his fine farm at the fort: here his crops of all kinds are very good, the grass excellent.

I next embarked on board a boat for the head of Hillsborough river, which is about eighteen miles. This river is from one quarter to a mile in breadth, and navigable for large vessels all along. The banks which are low, are very pleasant, particularly in some parts that are clear and houses built: along it are many large tracts of meadow, very rank. Near the head of the river the French had cleared a great deal of ground, which is now covered very thick with long grass. From the head of this river are nine miles to St Peter's, along a very level country, clear in some parts, and the grass so long, that it was with difficulty I could get along. About St Peter's,[70] which was the principal settlement the French had upon this island, there is a great deal of clear land, and the finest pasture I have seen. Mr Burns has several thousand acres of clear land, very flat; upon all this he has not above a hundred head of cattle, and as many sheep, with a few horses, where he might sufficiently keep ten times the quantity. Here is a good harbour, but not above eight or nine feet water over the bar; it runs several miles thro' the island, and is navigable in two different branches, or rivers, the one coming from the east, the other from the south: These rivers are well supplied with trout, eels, and some salmon, &c.

Returning again to Charlotte-town, I viewed several plantations by the way, at one of which I saw the best onions a-taking up that I have ever seen. The crops of wheat were generally pretty good; that sown in the fall, was universally the best: their barley is mostly of the naked or Siberia kind, which seems to agree well with this country: oats also thrive very well here.

I next embarked for the Three Rivers,[71] a harbour and settlement upon the south east of the island. This settlement was begun and supported by Mr Montgomery, Lord Advocate for Scotland; it is an exceeding good harbour, having plenty of water, and is the soonest clear of ice in the spring of any one upon the island. Here is also reserved four or five thousand acres for building a town upon a point of land between two of these rivers, to be named *George Town*. The land that has been cleared here is good pasture, the soil pretty good; here are about forty families, Scots and French settled. A considerable fishery used to be carried on from this port, but by a failure in the company it is now much decayed.

Thus having, in a six weeks tour, seen every setlement of consequence on the island, I am to return again to the continent. This island in general has many natural advantages, it is situated near an

[70] Saint Pierre was the largest French village, having been founded in 1720 as the center for the fisheries. Warburton, *Prince Edward Island*, 25.

[71] Trois Rivières, St. Pierre, and Tracadie were French fishing hamlets before the English occupation. Warburton, *Prince Edward Island*, 30.

exceeding fine fishery all along its north coast, with many safe and convenient harbours for small vessels. Along the south-side of the island are many safe harbours for large vessels, and the island is almost every where cut with navigable rivers, or inlets of the sea, which must be of great advantage to the place, as no part of it will be above four or five miles from water carriage. The air is very pure and healthy, the summer and autumn very mild and agreeable; the winter generally sets in pretty severe about Christmas, (tho' not so severe as has been represented) about which time the snow generally falls, and lies two feet deep for perhaps near three months, at this season, when the north west wind blows, it is very cold and nipping, but when the wind is from any other quarter, it is generally mild, and any person may work without his coat. The harbours are also generally frozen up for three months, consequently all communication with other parts are stopt during that time. At this season they draw home their wood and hay upon sledges, by horses or oxen, and they travel themselves some times in little sledges drawn by dogs, with incredible swiftness.

During this time of the year, as the settlement is but yet in its infancy, new settlers have been ill off for provisions, as few of their neighbours had any to spare, all having enough ado to support their own families; but the worst time for that is over, as the first settlers can now spare a little; yet I would advise settlers who go there, to take a year's provisions along with them.

Their cattle are of a very good kind, and neat; some of them weigh from seventy to eighty stone; their horses are the Canadian breed, about fourteen hands high, very handsome, and mettled; they have pretty good sheep and plenty of swine; they have no troublesome creatures upon the island, except bears, which some times fall upon their sheep or pigs in the woods. They are every where supplied with excellent water: and have no Indians to disturb them. They are a good deal troubled with musketoes, and small flies, in the summer and autumn; but as the island clears these decrease. They have a governor and council appointed by his Majesty, and an assembly chosen by the people: these meet annually at Charlotte-town, and enact laws in the same way as in the other colonies. Their laws are the same here as in Nova Scotia; but their specie is very scarce; they generally pay their labourers and trades-people in produce, such as wheat, oats, barley or cattle: they also draw bills which pass from one to another.

Cattle and provisions sell in this island about the following rates, *viz.* A horse, £ 10 or 12; a cow, about £ 6; A sheep, fourteen or fifteen shillings; beef, three pence halfpenny *per* pound; mutton, the same; salt pork, sixpence *per* pound; butter, nine or ten pence *per* pound; flour, twenty shillings *per* hundred weight; bisket, the same; potatoes, eighteen or twenty pence *per* bushel; cabbages, three pence a-piece; milk, two pence halfpenny a chopin, or quart; porter, forty five shillings *per* barrel. A labourer gets from eighteen pence to two shillings *per* day; a mason, three shillings *per* day; a joiner, the same, &c. all Halifax currency.

LETTER VI.

Philadelphia and Elizabeth town, 1775

From St John's I embarked for the continent again, and landed at Pictou, whence I traversed the wilds of Nova Scotia in the month of December; on this journey in company with two other itinerants, I lodged four nights in the woods, amongst the howlings of wild beasts, and the crashing of trees and wood peckers, and arrived at Halifax the 13th of December, whence, after staying a few days, I embarked on board a schooner for Philadelphia; and having a stormy passage, made Cape May the tenth day; and after lying off and on all night we hung out a signal for a pilot who soon came aboard. The mouth of Delaware from Cape May to Cape —— [Henlopen][72] light-house is about eight miles broad, having Maryland upon the south-west, and the Jerseys on the north-east: In it are many shoals, and the navigation dangerous without a pilot. All the way along the river, the banks, which are generally very low, make a fine appearance, with country houses, orchards, villages and fields interspersed: and in about sixteen hours we reached Philadelphia, which is about 150 miles up the river, it being late, we had but an imperfect view of Newcastle, Chester, Darby, &c. towns situated on the banks of the Delaware, below this city.

We arrived along side one of the quays a little after midnight, and were soon amused by hearing the watch call one o'clock thro' several parts of the city.[73] The situation of this city is very pleasant between two rivers, the Schuylkill on the west, and Delaware on the east. The plan, when compleat, is to fill the whole space between these two rivers, which are two miles distant, and to extend above two miles in length; but what is already compleated extends for about two miles and a half along the Delaware.[74] The streets running parralel

---

[72] M'Robert was always careful to verify names, and when he could not do so, he omitted them.

[73] As the result of public pressure, a paid watch was established in the city by an Act of the Assembly, in 1751. *Pennsylvania Statutes at Large* (17 vols., Harrisburg, 1896–1915), V. 111–128. In 1772 the watch was instructed to patrol the streets from 10 P.M. to 4 A.M., and call out the time of night and state of the weather. *Ibid.,* VIII. 96–115.

[74] Birket, in 1750, believed Philadelphia to be "perhaps one of the best Laid out Citys in the world and if built According to the Plan [of William Penn] wood be large enough for the Head of an Empire." *Some Cursory Remarks,* 63.

to that river are nine in number; these are crossed at right angles by twenty more, which are to run from one river to the other (which are both navigable) by which the city is divided into a number of regular squares. The streets are all straight, and well paved, about thirty-six or thirty-eight feet wide, with a foot path on every side, raised a little above the horse and carriage way, and laid with bricks for the conveniency of foot passengers:[75] they are tolerably well lighted with lamps in the winter,[76] and extremely well supplied with good water from pumps sunk at regular distances,[77] and are in many parts agreeably shaded with trees in the summer; under whose shade the inhabitants sit and do business or regale themselves.

The middle street that extends between the two rivers is one hundred feet wide,[78] and has a market place raised upon pillars, and covered over for a quarter of a mile in length: this market is supplied plentifully with all kinds of provisions.[79]

The buildings are mostly all brick, and very neat, three and four stories high, well finished within, and well lighted.

The publick buildings are spacious, and convenient, and some even elegant, especially the churches, the work-house,[80] court-house,[81] jail

[75] The streets were ordered paved by the Assembly in 1762, and the work was well done. *Pennsylvania Statutes at Large,* VI. 196–214; Miscellaneous Papers: Philadelphia Co. (Accounts of the Paving Commissioners, 1771–72), in THE HISTORICAL SOCIETY OF PENNSYLVANIA.

[76] "Monday Night last the Streets of this City began to be illuminated with Lamps in Pursuance of a late act of Assembly." *Pennsylvania Gazette,* October 3, 1751; *Pennsylvania Statutes at Large,* V. 111–128.

[77] A good account of these pumps and the controversies over them may be found in a broadside, "To the Inhabitants of Philadelphia," in the Gilpin Library, Vol. I. no. 139, THE HISTORICAL SOCIETY OF PENNSYLVANIA.

[78] High, or Market Street.

[79] The market had been rebuilt and greatly enlarged in 1773. *Minutes of the Common Council of the City of Philadelphia, 1704–1776.* (Philadelphia, 1847), 778. Josiah Quincy reported in 1773: "The Philadelphians boast of their market; it is undoubtedly the best regulated on the continent." *Memoir of the Life of Josiah Quincy, Junior* (2d. ed., Boston, 1874), 107.

[80] The famous Stone Prison (workhouse and house of correction), was erected at Sixth Street and Walnut in 1774, at a cost of £ 25,000, Pennsylvania currency. *Pennsylvania Statutes at Large,* VIII. 300–304.

[81] By court house M'Robert may have meant either the city hall, in Market Street, or the Colony House, at Sixth Street and Chestnut. The latter, of course, was one of the most beautiful buildings in the colonies; it was erected in 1742 according to plans drawn by Andrew Hamilton.

and hospital,[82] which are all fine buildings. The college is a tolerable edifice,[83] but not answerable to the others; here are also convenient barracks for, I believe, a thousand men.[84]

They have three English, and three Presbyterian churches, three Quakers meetings, two Methodists meetings, with several other places of worship belonging to other sectaries. Tho' the city is not above ninety years old the inhabitants are said to be about forty thousand.[85]

The quays and store-houses along the river side are very convenient: the principal quay is two hundred feet wide, where a vessel of five hundred tons may lay her side.

To this port belongs a great number of shipping; their trade is very extensive, and what I have said of New York in point of trade, is equally applicable to this city, which even outdoes New York in many particulars.[86] They build here annually not less than twenty-five vessels, from two hundred to five hundred tons burden each.

They have made great advances in most of the British manufactories here, such as making most kinds of hard-ware, clocks, watches, locks, guns, flints, glass, stone-ware, nails, paper, cordage, cloth, &c. &c.[87]

Their markets are supplied with all the necessaries of life in great plenty, nearly at the same prices as I mentioned at New York: their

[82] The Pennsylvania Hospital was opened in 1752, and the conditions for admission are printed in the *Pennsylvania Gazette,* March 24, 1752. The building to which M'Robert refers was opened in December, 1756. J. T. Scharf and T. Westcott, *History of Philadelphia* (3 vols., Philadelphia, 1884), I. 244.

[83] The Academy of Philadelphia, later the University of Pennsylvania, founded in 1751. Scharf and Westcott, *History of Philadelphia,* I. 245.

[84] Built for the British Army during the French and Indian War (1757). See sketch of barracks in Scharf and Westcott, *History of Philadelphia,* I. 253.

[85] This figure is probably the most accurate one we possess, and checks closely with information in the possession of the editor.

[86] Philadelphia had the largest trade in the colonies at this date. Max Savelle, in his *George Morgan: Colony Builder* (New York, 1932), gives a good picture of the business of the port. See, especially, page 112.

[87] All these items were advertised in the local press, 1765–1776; consult particularly, *Pennsylvanische Staatsbote,* January 5, 1773; *Pennsylvania Packet,* April 13, 1771; *Pennsylvania Chronicle,* January 1, 1770; *Pennsylvania Gazette,* October 19, 1769. A market for the exclusive sale of home manufactures was opened at the time of the Stamp Act, and ran for several years. *Ibid.,* December 12, 1765.

beef is very good, so is their pork and poultry. They have also plenty of fresh fish and oysters.[88]

The disposition of the inhabitants is pretty much the same with that of the New Yorkers; only making a little allowance for the stiffness and formality of the Quakers, who are the most numerous sect here.[89]

The country round this is very pleasant and agreeable, finely interspersed with genteel country seats,[90] fields and orchards, for several miles round, and along both the rivers for a good many miles. The soil is a mixture of clay and sand, yields very good crops of wheat, Indian corn, barley, tobacco, &c. and good clover hay. The cattle here are pretty well made, larger than your galloways, but not so well haired; make excellent beef, as may be seen daily in the shambles. Their horses are very neat, round punches, generally between fourteen and fifteen hands high, very mettled; six of them make a very pretty team, many of which are to be seen in the city every day in waggons loaded from the country with wheat, &c. Their sheep are something of the mug kind, rather long legged, though both the wool and mutton are pretty good.

From Philadelphia I set out with reluctance along the banks of the Delaware, which is navigable for vessels of considerable burden for twenty miles above the city, and for small craft much higher. All along are many pleasant little towns or villages, with numbers of small craft upon the river. On this road the inns are very good, and every thing as genteel as on any publick road in England. The principal towns I passed are New Bristol, Trenton, Burdingtown,[91] and Burlington, all pleasant country towns: the last is the capital of West

[88] "For abundance and goodness of the provisions of every kind, especially of butcher's meat, no market in America exceeds that of Philadelphia. Fish, especially sea fish, is what is not so abundant. The city being situate at so great a distance from the sea, the fish must be carried there with some trouble. . . . In the season shads (aloses) are very abundant in the river and of great service to the poorer sort of people." Du Simitière Papers (Ridgway Branch, Library Company of Philadelphia), 1769.

[89] But the tone of society was becoming steadily more and more Anglican, and less restricted. Compare, Alexander Graydon, *Memoirs of a Life Chiefly Passed in Pennsylvania with the Last Sixty Years* (Edinburgh, 1822), 74-75; and L. B. Walker, ed., *The Burd Papers* (Pottsville, Pa., 1899), 27-28, 54.

[90] These country seats were magnificent estates, of which only a few remain today. In Fairmount Park are preserved Mount Pleasant, the seat of the MacPhersons and Benedict Arnold, and several other beautiful mansions.

[91] Bordentown, N. J.

Jersey, and sometimes the seat of the governor, and where the assemblies are kept alternately. My way next led me to Princetown, a fine healthy clean-looking town: here is a spacious college, where are taught humanity, mathematicks, natural philosophy, and divinity. Dr. Wotherspoon from Paisley is president.[92] This is accounted a very healthy place, has a fine extensive view of the country round, is forty five miles from Philadelphia, and about the same distance from New York. From this I travelled through twenty-two miles of very fine country to New Brunswick, a pleasant town situated upon —— [the Raritan] river, adorned with three steeples; from thence I went to Woodbridge, a pleasant country village; thence through seven miles of very fine country to Elizabeth-town, which is very pleasantly situated, and contains about four hundred houses, mostly very neat brick buildings. It is only about a mile from a landing place, and twenty-eight miles by water from New York.

Here I happened to see a peat-stack, which being so uncommon a thing in this country, I inquired after the owner, who, I found, had come from the north of Ireland. The moss whence he had taken these peats was about four acres in extent, and about four feet deep, below which was a bed of exceeding fine shell-marle, of which the owner of the moss did not know the use, but promised to try a little of it, after I had told him its qualities.[93] I found several mosses in other parts of America, but none of any great extent, nor did I ever see any heath or heather there.

The first settlers of this country having pretty large tracts, divided them among their children: these again were subdivided to the children of the second generation, and perhaps these again to the third, by which the whole country seems to be divided into very small farms, many of them so small, that the owners do not think them worth keeping, but often sell them, and travel some hundreds of miles back, and purchase large tracts for the price of their small farms, where they have room for their numerous families. The government is pretty much the same as in the other neighbouring colonies; the governor generally resides at Perth Amboy, the capital of East Jersey, situated on the south-west side of the harbour of New York, about thirty miles from that city by water; but sometimes he

[92] Dr. Witherspoon was president of the College of New Jersey, later Princeton, founded in 1746.

[93] That is, as a fertilizer.

resides, and the courts are kept, at Burlingtown, which, as I said
before, was the capital of West Jersey.

This province has no foreign trade, New York and Philadelphia
being their markets where they dispose of their produce, which consists of Indian corn, wheat, barley, cyder, lumber, iron, pot and
pearl-ashes, cattle, skins, &c.; and where they purchase all their
necessaries.

The whole province is computed to contain about one hundred and
sixty thousand inhabitants.[94] A good many of these about Perth
Amboy are of Scots extraction, being carried thither in the *Caledonia*,
one of the ships that were sent on the *Darien* expedition, and wrecked
here. The crew and passengers getting ashore settled in this part of
the country, which still retains the name of *Scots Plains*.

Their manner of travelling here in winter is very pleasant after
the snow falls, which being generally so deep that coaches or other
wheel-carriages cannot pass, they use sleighs or sledges, made light
with a seat on them like an open chair: in these they sit and drive
themselves with great rapidity. The young ladies and gentlemen are
so fond of this, as a diversion, that whenever the snow gives over
falling, tho' it be after sun-set, they will not wait till next day, but
have their sleigh yoked directly, and drive about without the least
fear of catching cold from the night air. Large parties of pleasure are
often formed amongst them, when perhaps ten or twelve sleighs will
drive in company (with four in each sleigh) to dine and drink tea, and
return in the evening. About New York this sleighing is much used,
and large parties of pleasure are often formed to drive to the country.
Within a few miles of the city there is a little bridge, at the passing of
which, the young gentleman always claims a kiss from the lady that
sits along with him; this is a part of the etiquette that is never
omitted. Should any of the party be a stranger to the custom, the
ladies themselves will take care some way or other to have him informed. No carriage goes with so easy a motion as these sleighs do,
having none of the jolting motion of a wheel-carriage; but much resembling the motion of what we used to call a shuggie-shew, or a
vessel before a fine wind.

[94] In 1776, Congress estimated the population at 150,000. Greene and Harrington,
American Population, 108.

LETTER VII.

Leaving Elizabeth-town, I embarked for New York, where I said some time, and thence took an excursion up the province 165 miles to Albany; from that to Shenactady, sixteen miles. This is a pleasant town, situated on the Mohawk river, and contains about 500 houses.[95] From this is carried on an extensive trade with the Indians, on [and] the back settlements: they send batteaus loaded with rum, sugar, molasses, coarse clothing, powder, shot, guns, flints, toys, &c. eight or nine hundred miles up the river: these they exchange with the Indians for poultry [peltry?], furr, and some few conceits of Indian manufacture; such as belts, sashes, baskets, magazines, band-boxes, &c. This trade was formerly very advantageous; but the Indians of late are much wiser, and not so easily hoodwinked as formerly; still it continues a profitable branch of trade, till the late unhappy contest with the mother country has ruined all trade in these parts.

About forty miles above Shenactady, is Johnston,[96] a country town, and the seat of colonel Guy Johnston superintendant of Indian affairs: his father, Sir William, who died lately, much lamented, kept a vast influence amongst the Indians, which it is hoped his son will still maintain. About this place are several Indian towns, where they have some cows, cultivate some corn, and imitate the European settlers; but they still retain so much of their former disposition, *viz.* an aversion to labour, and an itch for roving from place to place, that they are not likely soon, if ever, to make good farmers. Here the soil is very good, and the timber large, but of no farther use than for fire, farming utensils, and fencing, being too far from a market to be exported, and the falls in the Mohawk river prevent their sending it by water to Albany, or New York.[97] About this time of year, March settlers are busy making their sugar, which they extract from the mapple tree thus; they cut a notch slanting across the tree, about two or three feet from the ground, in the lower end of that notch they fix a little spout or trough to carry the juices of the tree that come out at the notch down to a vessel or trough placed

---

[95] In 1769 Richard Smith estimated that Albany contained 300 houses. Greene and Harrington, *American Population*, 102n.

[96] Johnson Hall, in the Mohawk Valley.

[97] As early as 1771 there was considerable agitation for improving the navigation on the Mohawk. *New York Weekly Mercury*, August 26, 1771.

at the foot of the tree to receive it; these juices are carried to a large
pot or boiler fixed or hung up in the wood in a convenient place,
where they may fetch the juices of fifty or sixty trees they will have
all notched at once; when they have their pot or boiler full, they put
a large fire to it, and with about ten hours constant boiling, they
reduce it to sugar; about four gallons of the juice will afford a pound
of sugar; this sugar is very agreeable to the taste, accounted very
wholesome, of a brownish collour, and a little tough, resembling
gum.

This, as I believe most of the back countries of America, are all
given away in large grants from ten to a hundred thousand acres;
these the proprietors dispose of, as they best can, in small lots, either
selling or leasing them out: the terms are very different, and depend
greatly upon the situation: if near a navigable river, they are higher,
and diminish in proportion to the distance. For example, woodlands
on the Mohawk river will sell from five to ten shillings *per* acre;
those three miles distant, under five shillings; those seven or eight
miles, at about two shillings; and, at ten miles from the river, they
may be bought at one and sixpence sterling *per* acre. Cleared land,
with houses or other improvements, are sold in proportion to what
the value of woodland was before cleared, adding what they think
has been expended on improvement. Woodlands are rented, on the
river for four years free, after that to pay sixpence *per* acre for ever:
those farther back, cheaper in proportion to their distance. In some
parts, the leases are for ever, in others, for ninety nine, and sixty
years; and some for three lives; the rents are paid in some parts in
wheat, ten Winchester bushels to the hundred acres, in other parts,
as high as twenty bushels *per* hundred acres.

Population makes an amazing progress in all these countries. It
has been computed by those who have been minute in inquiries of
that kind, that the number of inhabitants have doubled in fifteen or
sixteen years; I cannot say how far these calculations are right, but
I am persuaded, that the increase is prodigious; it is no uncommon
thing to see a mother of thirteen or fourteen years of age, and it is
rare to see a maid unmarried at eighteen. They generally have many
children, the country houses swarm with them.[98]

[98] According to the census of 1771, the province of New York contained 168,007
inhabitants; in 1776 estimates placed the number at 190,000. Greene and Harrington,
American Population, 91, 91*n*.

The ease with which people can maintain a family, induces the young men to marry very young; one may see many young couples married and set up for themselves here, whose ages put together would not make above thirty years. This I think is a very clear proof of a happy country.

The houses in the back settlements are generally all built of logs at first, which when they take pains to square and lay right, make very good houses for many years: but the new settlers are generally in such a hurry to get up their houses, that they pile up round trees one above another, notching them at the corners to hinder them from falling, saw out a door and windows, and bind a roof, covering it with bark instead of shingles, and plaistering up the joints between the trees with clay and straw: with these they put up for some years, till they find leisure and ability to build better.

Lower down upon Hudson's or Delaware rivers, the land sells or lets higher; woodland lying on these rivers, will sell from ten to twenty shillings *per* acre: a few miles off the river for about ten shillings, &c. Near New York or Philadelphia, thro' the Jerseys, and Long Island, the land is all settled, and mostly cleared. Here-about lands sell as high as £ 5. sterling *per* acre, and if in a very good situation or near the cities, a good deal higher. I know land within a mile of New York rented at £ 3. currency *per* acre, and the same near Philadelphia.

The lands about Newport, on Rhode Island, let at about a doller an acre, and sell from twelve to twenty years purchase.

In Nova Scotia, the rates of land are lower than of most of those I have mentioned; by applying to the governor, one may have very good woodland there near a navigable river for paying sixpence sterling *per* acre purchase money, and subject to a quit-rent of two shillings *per* hundred acres for ever.

Woodlands may be bought in the Island of St John's[99] from one shilling to five shillings *per* acre, subject to quit-rents, which are from two shillings to six shillings *per* hundred acres. This quit-rent is hard upon many of the proprietors who have got little or none of their lots settled. The climate of this large country varies in different places, but in general it is healthy, and agrees well with European constitutions, which I may say from experience.

[99] Prince Edward Island.

It is very hot about Philadelphia and New York, &c. for about two months, *viz*. July and August; after that the weather is very agreeable and fine, till about Christmass, or New-year's day, when the snow generally falls, and a hard frost sets in, and continues (but always clear and serene) till March; then the snows go off: and in April a fine spring sets suddenly in. It is amazing to see the change that is here in a few days; trees, flowers, plants, &c. all get on their green livery, and the whole vegetable world seem to vie with one another. You cannot fancy a more agreeable scene than to be sailing on one of these rivers, hung on every side with fruit trees in full bloom. Nothing can equal the delicious fragrance, or beautiful appearance that is every where to be met with at this season of the year.

This agreeable weather continues till about the first of July; only this profusion of blossoms is succeeded by as great a profusion of fruits; at that time, as I said before, it begins to grow too hot.

They have not near so much rain as you have in Britain; by this you would imagine that they are much burnt up with drought, which is not the case, for the length of the nights in the summer, together with the heavy dews, prevents this.

They have frequent thunders in the summer and harvests, with sudden showers of rain. The air is very full of lightning, which used to do frequent damage to their houses; but they have mostly all got conductors, which I need not inform you, are a spike of iron fixed upon the highest part of the building, and carried down along the side of the wall till it enter the ground. These are found by experience to attract the fire, and conduct it down to the earth, whereby most of the damage that used to be sustained that way is prevented.[100]

Lead is also found by experience to be a conductor; so that where they have lead spouts, they generally bring the iron spike to join the lead; from thence they carry the lead into the ground, which answers all the purposes of a conductor. In hopes of having further opportunities of learning their laws, customs, &c. I have purposely avoided mentioning to you any thing of the Indians or ancient inhabitants of this country, who are yet almost in a state of nature; their manners unimproved, and also uncorrupted by what we call polite education, or the science of vice. These are a tall, nimble, well-

[100] It is interesting to note the widespread use of Franklin's recent invention.

made people; many of tham about six feet high, with long black hair, their complexion a little tawny, or copper-coloured; their eyes black and piercing, their features good, especially the women. They live chiefly by hunting, fishing, and upon fruits. Their clothing is generally a skin or blanket, made with sleeves like a short jocky-coat, and tied about the waist with a belt. The women have some of them a short petticoat reaching to the knee; few of them have any shirts, nor have the men any breeches. They have stockings laced up the outside of the leg, and shoes made of deer, mouse or sea-cow skin, all of one piece, and laced above the foot with thongs of leather. Many of them wear no clothes in the summer; only the women wear a piece of skin or cloth about their middle. They are very fond of beads, ear-rings, feathers, or other shewy toys, to adorn their head and neck, and are sometimes at great pains in curious plaiting up their hair, adorning it with feathers, &c. They live in huts called *Wigwams*, which they will erect in a few hours thus: They drive in two forked sticks into the ground, and place a roof between them; then lay some sticks from the ground slanting in both sides like rafters; these sticks they cover with bark of trees, branches, or skins of wild beasts, so as to keep out the rain; in the midst of this they kindle their fire, and lie round it upon fir-tops, skins, or any thing they can get. They seldom stay long in one place, but are frequently shifting, wherever they think the game, fishes, or fruits most plenty: They carry all their furniture upon their back, which consists of a gun, a tomahawk, a powder-horn, a steel and flint, a pipe and tobacco, a vessel to boil their meat in, with perhaps some few toys.

No beings seem to enjoy more contentment of peace of mind than they do, nor live more social or happy among themselves. They are great epicures when they have any varieties, and are very fond of rum or other spirituous liquors. I am apt to question the reality of the various accounts of their vindictive and implacable temper, and hatred of their neighbours the European settlers, except in cases where the Europeans are the first aggressors: on the contrary, I believe the Indians are naturally good-natured, and obliging, when they are not ill-used; but when, by bad treatment, they are obliged to take up the hatchet, they are a cruel enemy indeed. They are very docile and tractable, and learn any thing fast that they wish to acquire.[101]

They are very curious in making many conceits from shells, feathers, the bark of trees, &c. They plait or weave a kind of cloth from a weed that grows in this country. The construction of their bark canoes is curious, being made of the bark of the birch tree sewed together. These will float in four inches water, and will carry twelve or fourteen men, and when they come to any shoals or rocks that they cannot pass, two of them will get her up on their shoulders, and carry her perhaps some miles, to a place where they can launch her again.

Were I an able naturalist, I might have given you a description of the different species of animals, birds, serpents, reptiles, &c. to be found in this large country; but this being beyond my abilities, and far exceeding the narrow bounds I am here confined to, I shall not attempt it, nor need I give you a catalogue of their names, as you may see that elsewhere in books upon that subject: or were I an arborist or florist, I would have described and analized to you the many species of trees, shrubs, flowers, &c to be found here; but these, with many other particulars, that a more able and more curious observer might fill a volume with, I shall pass over in silence, for fear of exposing further my own ignorance and inability.

You may also be surprised that I say nothing of the unhappy contest now subsisting between this and the mother country: This I leave to politicians; but am afraid both parties will repent when too late their having launched so inconsiderately into it. When it will end, God only knows, I fear the ruin of one, if not of both countries. Many fine industrious families, lately in affluence now do not know where to turn to avoid the dreadful stroke of a desolating war: all is confusion. This is the last you need expect from me from this side of the water, as I intend soon to revisit my native country till we see better times, which I wish may be soon.

New York, May,   I am, &c.
1775

---

[101] M'Robert here bases his observations upon the three groups of natives with which he had come into contact: the Iroquois, Micmacs, and Delawares.

RATES of the STAGES
from
New York to Philadelphia.

The flying machine,[102] sets out from Powles-hook, opposite to New York, for Philadelphia, every Monday, Wednesday, and Friday morning in summer; from November first, to May first, it performs the journey only twice a-week, and sets out on Mondays and Thursdays. The waggons from Philadelphia set off the same mornings. As the Machines set off from Powles-hook early in the morning, passengers should cross the ferry the evening before.

The price for each passenger is twenty shillings currency. In snowy weather in winter, they use sleighs or sledges, instead of wheel-machines. They change horses only once at Prince-town.

The boat sets out from Whitehall-slip in New York, on Mondays and Thursdays, and the passengers generally arrive at Philadelphia on Wednesdays and Saturdays following.

	£.	s.	d.
For a passenger from New York to Amboy,.............	o:	2:	o
From Perth Amboy to Bordentown in the waggon	o:	5:	o
From Bordentown to Philadelphia [by boat]............	o:	1:	6

From Bordentown to Philadelphia for goods.	£.	s.	d.
From New York to Amboy *per* cwt...................	o:	1:	o
From Amboy to Bordentown *per* cwt...................	o:	2:	9
From Bordentown to Philadelphia *per* cwt..............	o:	1:	o
From Amboy to Burlington in a waggon,...............	o:	6:	o
From Burlington to Philadelphia in a boat,.............	o:	1:	o
Goods from Amboy to Burlington *per* cwt. in the waggon,.	o:	3:	3
From Burlington to Philadelphia in ditto...............	o:	o:	6
All New York currency.			

Duties paid in New York, by act of assembly on goods imported.

All wines, *per* pipe, twenty seven shillings. Rum, shrub, and all sorts of spirituous liquors, two pence *per* gallon. Negroes, if directly from Africa, forty shillings *per* head; and if from any other place, eighty shillings.

Dry goods from the West Indies, or any colony on the continent, pay five *per cent.* of their value.

[102] In 1774, John Mercereau advertised his stage coach, "The Flying Machine," to run between Paulus Hook Ferry and the Indian Queen Tavern, Philadelphia, in two days' time: thirty shillings "in Coach," and twenty shillings for "outside Passengers." *New York Weekly Mercury*, January 3, 1774.

VALUE AND WEIGHT OF COINS AS THEY NOW PASS IN THE FOLLOWING PROVINCES.

		Sterling.	New York.	Least weight.	Connecticut.	Philadelphia.	Quebeck, &c.	Nova Scotia, & St John's Island.
		£ s. d.	£ s. d.	dwt. gr.	£ s. d.	£ s. d.	£ s. d.	£ s. d.
Sterling.	Shilling,…………	0: 1: 0	0: 1: 9		0: 1: 4	0: 1: 6	0: 1: 4	0: 1: 2½
	Crown,……………	0: 5: 0	0: 8: 9		0: 6: 8	0: 7: 6	0: 6: 8	0: 5: 6½
	Guinea…………	1: 1: 0	1: 17: 0	5: 3	1: 8: 0	1: 14: 0	1: 8: 0	1: 3: 4
Spanish.	Pisterean,………		0: 1: 7		0: 1: 2½	0: 1: 4	0: 1: 2	
	Dollar,……………	0: 4: 6	0: 8: 0	17: 6	0: 6: 0	0: 7: 6	0: 6: 0	0: 5: 0
	Pistole,…………	0: 16: 6	1: 9: 0	4: 8	1: 2: 0	1: 7: 0	1: 1: 0	
	Doubloon,………		5: 16: 0	17: 8	4: 8: 0	5: 8: 6	4: 4: 0	
Portugal.	Moidore,…………	1: 7: 0	2: 8: 0	6: 8	1: 16: 0	2: 3: 6	1: 16: 0	
	*Half Johannes,…	1: 16: 0	3: 4: 0	9: 0	2: 8: 0	3: 0: 0	2: 8: 0	2: 0: 0
French.	Crown,……………	0: 5: 0	0: 8: 6		0: 6: 8	0: 7: 6	0: 6: 8	0: 5: 6
	Pistole,…………	0: 16: 0	1: 8: 0	4: 5	1: 0: 0	1: 6: 6	1: 1: 0	
	Louis d'Or,……	1: 1: 0	1: 16: 0	5: 4		1: 13: 0	1: 8: 0	
German.	Caroline………		1: 18: 0	6: 8		1: 14: 0	1: 10: 0	

* At a meeting of the Chamber of Commerce, Aug. 7, 1770, it was resolved, that the members of that corporation at New York, would in future pay and receive all Half Johannes that weigh nine penny weight, at £ 3: 4: 0, and for every grain they weigh more allow three pence *per* grain, and for every grain they weigh less, deduct four pence.

LIST OF ROADS IN NORTH AMERICA.

Roads, South-west from New York.

	Miles.	Miles.
To Newark, part by water	9	
Elizabeth-town	6	15
Wood-bridge	10	25
Brunswick	10	35
Prince-town	17	52
Trenton	13	65
Bristol	10	75
Frankford	15	90
Philadelphia	5	95
Darby	7	102
Chester,	9	111
Barandiwine[103]	14	125
Newcastle	6	131
Elk River	17	148
North-east	7	155
Susquehanna	9	164
Gunpowder Ferry	25	189
Patapsco Ferry	20	209
Annapolis in Maryland	30	239
Mount Pleasant	13	252
Upper Marlboro'	9	261
Piscataway	15	276
Port Tobacco'	15	291
Hose's Ferry	10	301
Port Royal	15	316
Snead's Tavern	12	328
Todd's Bridge	20	348
Caleborn's Bridge	24	372
Ferneaus	12	384
Williamsburg	16	400
Hog Island	7	407
Isle of Wight	18	425
Nansemond	20	445
Bennet's Creek	30	475
Edinton[104]	30	505
Bell's Ferry	8	513
Bath-town	45	558
Neuse River	32	590
Whittock River	20	610
New River	30	640
Cape Fear river	45	685
East end of Long Bay	45	730
West end of ditto	25	755
George-town	30	785
Santee Ferry	12	797
Sawee Ferry	20	814
Charlestown, South Carolina	30	847

[817]

[103] Brandywine.
[104] Edenton, N. C.

Roads from New York to Canada.

	Miles.	Miles.
To King's-bridge	15	
Conklins	12	27
Bernard's	12	39
Peck's-kill	10	49
Rodger's, Highlands	9	58
Fish Kills	11	69
Poughkeepsie	14	83
Staatsburgh	11	94
Rynbeck	6	100
Shermerhorns	10	110
Livingston's Manor	14	124
Claverack	7	131
Kinderhook	14	145
Half-way-house	10	155
Albany	10	165
Saratoga	36	201
Fort Edward	20	221
Lake George	14	235
Ticonderoga	30	265
Crown Point	15	280
Willsborough	20	300
Fort St John's, north end of Lake Champlain	68	368
Le Praire	15	383
Montreal	6	389
Trois Rivieres	90	479
Quebeck	80	559

Road to Boston from New York.

	Miles.	Miles.
To King's-bridge	15	
East Chester	6	21
N. Rochell	4	25
Rye	5	30
Horse-neck	6	36
Standford	7	43
Norwalk	10	53
Fairfield	12	65
Stratford	8	73
Milford	4	77
New Haven	10	87
Wallingford	13	100
Durham	7	107
M. Town[105]	6	113
Weathers-field	11	124
Hartford	3	127
Windsor	8	153
Enfield	8	143
Springfield	10	153
Kingston	15	168
Western	9	177

[105] Middletown, Conn.

	Miles.	Miles.
Brookfield..	6	183
Spencer..	8	191
Leicester...	6	197
Worcester..	6	203
Shrewsbury...	5	208
Marlborough..	10	218
Sudbury..	11	229
Water-town...	10	239
Boston...	10	249

Post Road on Long Island, from New York.

	Miles.	Miles.	
Jamaica..	12		
Capt. Plat...	13	25	
Huntington...	15	40	
Blindbury's...	15	55	
Satauket...	10	56	[65]
Wading River..	16	81	
River-head...	11	92	
Hubbard's..	10	102	
Shelter Isle Ferry....................................	12	114	
Hog Neck..	4	118	
Sag-harbour Ferry....................................	4	122	
East Hampton..	7	129	
South Hampton.......................................	14	143	
Homan's Tavern......................................	16	159	
Smiths...	9	168	
Dunbarrs...	9	177	
Avery's Tavern.......................................	9	186	
Morris's..	6	192	
Udell's...	17	209	
Waters's..	13	222	
Hampstead Tavern....................................	7	229	
Jamaica again..	10	239	

Distances to the Mississippi.

	Miles.	Miles.	
From Louisburg to Quebeck............................	360		
Trois Rivieres..	80	440	
Montreal..	90	530	
La Galatte...	120	650	
Fort Frontenac.......................................	90	740	
Oswego across the east end of lake Ontario............	60	800	
Niagara Falls...	160	960	
A store-house...	20	980	
Lake Erie..	10	990	
Fort Presque Isle.....................................	90	1080	
Beauf River[106]......................................	15	1095	
Pittsburg...	180	1215	[1275]
Ohio Falls..	600	1815	[1875]
Mississippi...	300	2115	[2175]
Mouth of ditto.......................................	930	3045	[3105]

FINIS.

[106] Rivière aux Boeufs: the present Venango River, in Pennsylvania.

INDEX

New York, city of, animals of, 6; buildings, 3–4; fire defenses, 4; inhabitants, 5; prostitutes, 5; streets, 4–5; trade, 2, 5, 34; water supply, 4; wharves, 1–2.

New York Bay, 1.

Newcastle, Pa., 29.

Newport, R. I., buildings, 13; description, 13, 14; trade, 14.

Nova Scotia, climate, 22; currency, 18; description of, 22; population, 21; soil, 21–22.

Peat, use of in N. J., 33.

Pennsylvania, province of, animals, 32; crops, 32; soil, 32.

Perth Amboy, N. J., 33.

Philadelphia, Pa., 29, 34; buildings, 30–31; commerce, 31; manufacturing at, 31; markets, 31–32; night watch, 29; plan of, 29–30.

Philadelphians, character of, 32.

Pictou, N. S., 21, 29.

Prince Edward Island, advantages of, 26–27; climate, 27; crops, 26; livestock, 27; trade and prices at, 27–28.

Princeton, N. J., 33.

Princeton, college at, 33.

Prince-Town, P. E. I., 24–25.

Raritan River, 33.

Rhode Island, island of, 11; animals, 14; crops, 13.

Rhode Island, province of, currency, 14; government, 14; inhabitants, 16.

St John's Island.
    See Prince Edward Island.

St. Peter's, P. E. I., 26.

Sandy Hook, 1.

Schenectady, N. Y., fur and Indian trade, 35.

Soil, at Albany, 8.

Stage rates, N. Y. to Phila., 41.

Staten Island, 1.

Stewiacke River, 20.

Three Rivers, P. E. I., 26.

Tracadie, P. E. I., 25.

Travel, methods in Middle Colonies, 24.

Trenton, N. J., 32.

Truro, N. S. *See* Cobiquid.

Wages of laborers, at N. Y., 9; at Prince Edward Island, 28.

West New Jersey, 34.

Windsor, N. Y., 7.

Woodbridge, N. J., 33.